To
From
Date
D1021979

Little Messengers of Hope
Artwork by
Carolyn Shores Wright
HARVEST HOUSE PUBLISHERS
EUGENE, OREGON

Little Messengers of Hope

Published by Harvest House Publishers
Eugene, Oregon 97402
www.harvesthousepublishers.com

ISBN 978-0-7369-2482-5

Design and production by Garborg Design Works, Savage, Minnesota

Printed in China

11 12 13 14 15 / LP / 10 9 8 7

Beautiful and
graceful, varied and
enchanting, small
but approachable,
butterflies lead you to
the sunny side of life.
And everyone deserves
a little sunshine.

JEFFREY GLASSBERG

What the caterpillar calls the end of the world, the master calls a butterfly.

Richard Bach

We judge of

man's wisdom by his hope.

RALPH WALDO EMERSON

I choose to rise up out of that storm and see that in moments of desperation, fear, and helplessness, each of us can be a rainbow of hope, doing what we can to extend ourselves in kindness and grace to one another. And I know for sure that there is no them…there's only us.

OPRAH WINFREY

*And now these three remain:
faith, hope and love.*

THE BOOK OF 1 CORINTHIANS

Always look out for the sunlight
the Lord sends into your days.

HOPE CAMPBELL

*Optimism is the faith that leads
to achievement. Nothing can be done
without hope and confidence.*

HELEN KELLER

Hope is like the sun, which,
as we walk toward it, casts a
shadow of our burdens behind us.

AUTHOR UNKNOWN

Hope is both the
earliest and the most
indispensable virtue
inherent in the state of
being alive. If life is to
be sustained hope must
remain, even where
confidence is wounded,
trust impaired.

ERIK H. ERIKSON

The word which God has written

Hope is some extraordinary spiritual grace that God gives us to control our fears, not to oust them.

VINCENT MCNABB

on the brow of every man is Hope.

VICTOR HUGO

Now faith is the
substance of things
hoped for, the evidence
of things not seen.
THE BOOK OF HEBREWS

Soft as the voice of an angel,
Breathing a lesson unheard,
Hope with a gentle persuasion
Whispers her comforting word:

Wait till the darkness is over,
Wait till the tempest is done,
Hope for the sunshine tomorrow,
After the shower is gone.

SEPTIMUS WINNER
"Whispering Hope"

They say a person needs just three things to be truly happy in this world. Someone to love, something to do, and something to hope for.

TOM BODETT

We delight in the beauty of
the butterfly, but rarely
admit the changes it has gone
through to achieve that beauty.

MAYA ANGELOU

Hope is the parent of faith.

CYRUS A. BARTOL

Hope is a strange invention—
A Patent of the Heart—
In unremitting action
Yet never wearing out.

EMILY DICKINSON

Never be in a hurry; do everything quietly and in a calm spirit. Do not lose your inward peace for anything whatsoever, even if your whole world seems upset. Commend all to God, and then lie still and be at rest in His bosom.

St. Frances de Sales

Our brightest blazes of gladness are commonly kindled by unexpected sparks.

Samuel Johnson

Today a new sun rises for me;
everything lives...
everything invites me to cherish it.

Anne de Lenclos

Confidence in the love of God
envelops us with the fragrance
of faith, hope, and love.

SANDY CLOUGH

What oxygen is to the lungs, such

But, as you know, my heart is usually brimful of happiness. The thought that my dear Heavenly Father is always near, giving me abundantly of all those things which truly enrich my life and make it sweet and beautiful, makes every deprivation seem of little moment compared with the countless blessings I enjoy.

HELEN KELLER

is hope to the meaning of life.

EMIL BRUNNER

Hope is a state of mind, not of the world. Hope, in this deep and powerful sense, is not the same as joy that things are going well, or willingness to invest in enterprises that are obviously heading for success, but rather an ability to work for something because it is good.

VACLAV HAVEL

Hope is a risk that must be run.

GEORGES BERNANOS

Be joyful in hope, patient

in affliction, faithful in prayer.

The Book of Romans

Jesus, my Strength, my Hope,
On Thee I cast my care,
With humble confidence look up,
And know Thou hear'st my prayer.
Give me on Thee to wait
Till I can all things do;
On Thee, almighty to create,
Almighty to renew.

John Wesley

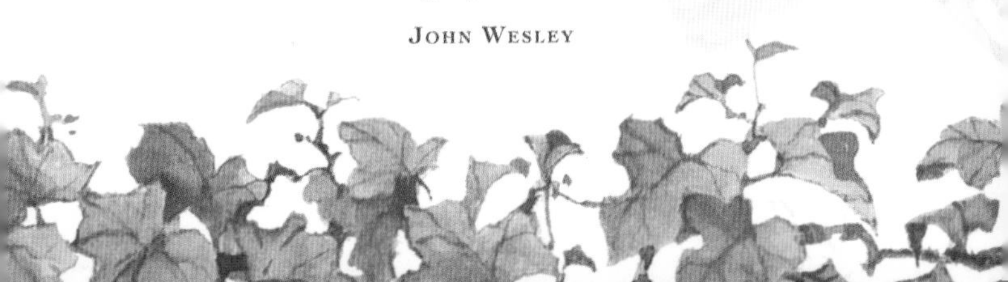

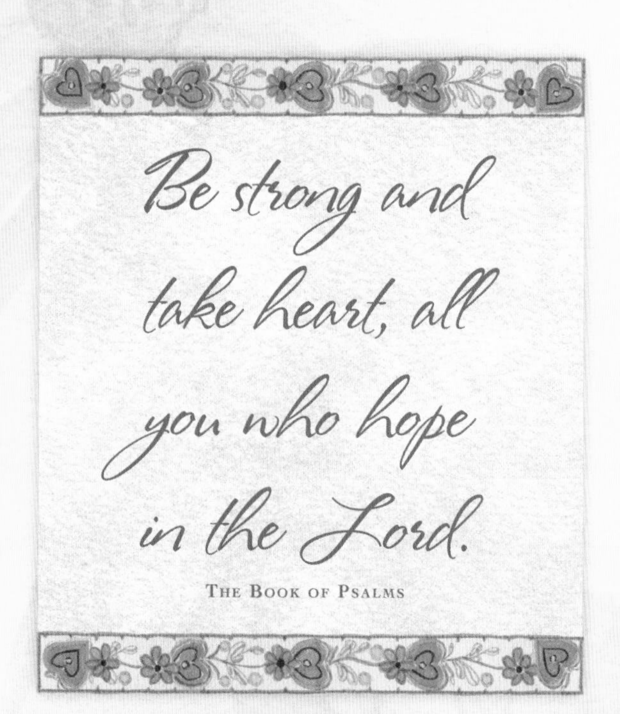
Be strong and
take heart, all
you who hope
in the Lord.
THE BOOK OF PSALMS

And thus, oh Hope! Thy lovely form
In sorrow's gloomy night shall be
The sun that looks through cloud and storm
Upon a dark and moonless sea.

JOSEPH RODMAN DRAKE

Hope is a thing with feathers
That perches in the soul,
And sings the tune without words
And never stops at all.

EMILY DICKINSON

Take short views,
hope for the best,
and trust in God.

SYDNEY SMITH

Hope sees the invisible, feels the intangible, and achieves the impossible.

AUTHOR UNKNOWN

Hope is a gift we give ourselves, and it remains when all else is gone.

NAOMI JUDD

Lord, make us mindful of the little things that grow and blossom in these days to make the world beautiful for us.

W.E.B. DU BOIS

Everything that is done in the

As long as we have hope, we have direction, the energy to move, and the map to move by. We have a hundred alternatives, a thousand paths, and an infinity of dreams. Hopeful, we are halfway to where we want to go; hopeless, we are lost forever.

AUTHOR UNKNOWN

Such is hope, heaven's
own gift to struggling
mortals, pervading, like
some subtle essence from
the skies, all things both
good and bad.

CHARLES DICKENS

world is done by hope.

MARTIN LUTHER

My hope arises from the freeness of grace,
and not from the freedom of the will.

CHARLES HADDON SPURGEON

*I thank you God for this most amazing day:
for the leaping greenly spirits of trees and for
the blue dream of sky and for everything which
is natural, which is infinite, which is yes.*

E. E. CUMMINGS

Hope is the pillar that holds up the world.
Hope is the dream of a waking man.

PLINY

We must accept
finite disappointment,
but never lose
infinite hope.
MARTIN LUTHER KING JR.

Hope is itself a species of happiness, and, perhaps, the chief happiness which this world affords.

SAMUEL JOHNSON

Anyone can count the number of seeds in an apple, but only God can count the number of apples in a seed.

ROBERT H. SCHULLER

Let nothing disturb thee,
Let nothing affright thee.
All things are passing.
God never changes.

St. Theresa de Avila

God stirs up our comfortable nests, and pushes us over the edge of them, and we are forced to use our wings to save ourselves from fatal falling. Read your trials in this light, and see if your wings are being developed.

Hannah Whitall Smith

*Happiness is a butterfly, which when pursued,
is always just beyond your grasp, but which,
if you will sit down quietly, may alight upon you.*

Nathaniel Hawthorne

Let perseverance be your engine and hope your fuel.

H. Jackson Brown Jr.

Every experience God gives us, every person
He puts in our lives, is the perfect preparation
for the future that only He can see.

Corrie ten Boom

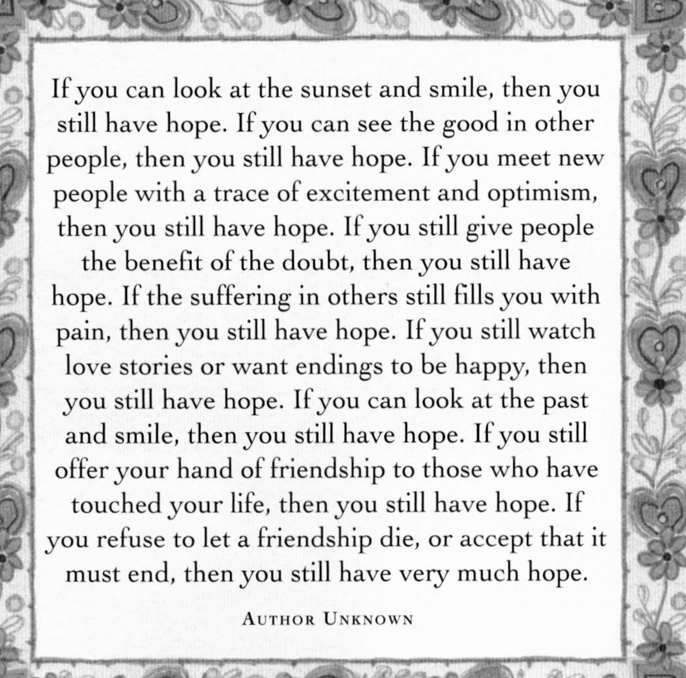

If you can look at the sunset and smile, then you still have hope. If you can see the good in other people, then you still have hope. If you meet new people with a trace of excitement and optimism, then you still have hope. If you still give people the benefit of the doubt, then you still have hope. If the suffering in others still fills you with pain, then you still have hope. If you still watch love stories or want endings to be happy, then you still have hope. If you can look at the past and smile, then you still have hope. If you still offer your hand of friendship to those who have touched your life, then you still have hope. If you refuse to let a friendship die, or accept that it must end, then you still have very much hope.

AUTHOR UNKNOWN

Hope is putting faith to work when doubting would be easier.

Author Unknown

We wait in hope for the LORD; he is our help and our shield. In him our hearts rejoice, for we trust in his holy name. May your unfailing love rest upon us, O LORD, even as we put our hope in you.

THE BOOK OF PSALMS

There is surely a future hope for you, and your hope will not be cut off.

THE BOOK OF PROVERBS

When the world says, "Give up," Hope whispers, "Try it one more time."

AUTHOR UNKNOWN

I will grant peace in the land, and you will lie down and no one will make you afraid.

THE BOOK OF LEVITICUS

Hope is faith holding out

its hand in the dark.

George Iles

How can God direct

Prayer increases our ability to accept the present moment. You cannot live in the future, you cannot live in the past, you can only live in the now. The present moment is already exactly as it ought be, even if we do not understand why it is as it is.

Matthew Kelly

Eternity is the divine treasure house, and hope is the window, by means of which mortals are permitted to see, as through glass darkly, the things which God is preparing.

William Mountford

our steps if we're not taking any?

Sarah Leah Grafstein

Let nothing come
Never fear shadows.
They simply mean
there's a light shining
somewhere nearby.
RUTH E. RENKEL

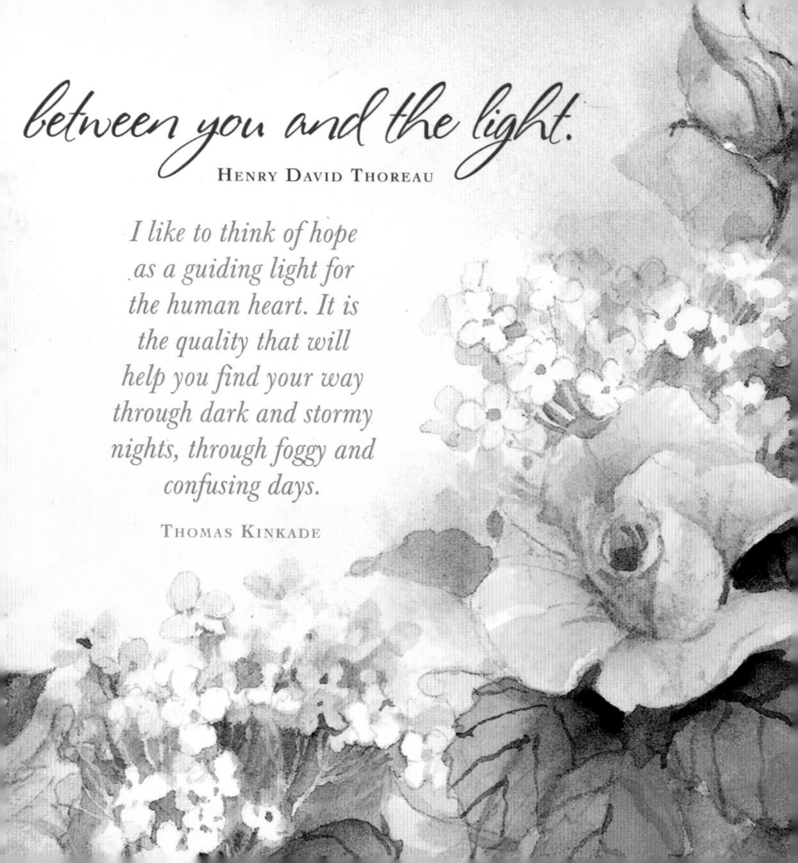
between you and the light.
HENRY DAVID THOREAU
I like to think of hope
as a guiding light for
the human heart. It is
the quality that will
help you find your way
through dark and stormy
nights, through foggy and
confusing days.
THOMAS KINKADE

Hope can see Heaven through

Hope is the confidence that even though more winters will surely come, even more certainly the roses will follow in an ever-increasing abundance.

Sandy Clough

Hope and patience are two sovereign remedies for all, the surest reposals, the softest cushions to lean on in adversity.

Robert Burton

the thickest clouds.
Thomas Brooks

Hope is

A little faith will bring your soul to heaven,
but a lot of faith will bring heaven to your soul.

Dwight L. Moody

May the God of hope fill you with all joy and peace as you trust in him, so that you may overflow with hope.

The Book of Romans

faith in the future tense.

Peter Anderson

Answered prayer is a testimony to God's unfailing faithfulness. I can say without a doubt that *prayer works!* If you will lift up the concerns of your heart in prayer as the Holy Spirit leads you and look to God to be the source of all you want to see happen in your life, great things will happen. Don't worry about *how* He will answer you, just know that you can rest in Him.

STORMIE OMARTIAN

Hope ever urges on and tells us tomorrow will be better.

TIBULLUS

Faith, like

Life's like a boomerang. The more good you throw out, the more you receive in return.

Josh S. Hinds

Those who bring sunshine
to the lives of others cannot
keep it from themselves.

James M. Barrie

a muscle, grows by stretching.

A.W. Tozer

My hope is built on nothing less
Than Jesus' blood and righteousness.
I dare not trust the sweetest frame,
But wholly trust in Jesus' Name.

On Christ the solid Rock I stand,
All other ground is sinking sand;
All other ground is sinking sand.

When darkness seems to hide His face,
I rest on His unchanging grace.
In every high and stormy gale,
My anchor holds within the veil.

His oath, His covenant, His blood,
Support me in the whelming flood.
When all around my soul gives way,
He then is all my Hope and Stay.

EDWARD MOTE
"My Hope Is Built"

Looking forward

to things is half the pleasure of them.

LUCY MAUD MONTGOMERY

It's all right to have butterflies in your stomach. Just get them to fly in formation.

ROB GILBERT

We may run, walk, stumble, drive, or fly, but let us never lose sight of the reason for the journey, or miss a chance to see a rainbow on the way.

GLORIA GAITHER

There is no medicine like hope, no incentive so great, and no tonic so powerful as expectation of something better tomorrow.

ORISON MARDEN

In the middle of difficulty lies opportunity.

ALBERT EINSTEIN

The inner half of every cloud
Is bright and shining;
I therefore turn my clouds about,
And always wear them inside out
To show the lining.

ELLEN THORNYCROFT FOWLER

Joy is a light that fills you with hope and faith and love.

ADELA ROGERS ST. JOHNS

The capacity for hope is the most significant fact of life. It provides human beings with a sense of destination and the energy to get started.

NORMAN COUSINS

Hope is passion for what

is possible.

Soren Kierkegaard

Once you choose hope, anything's possible.

Christopher Reeve